P9-DYD-128

May the God of hope fill you with all joy and peace in believing, so that by the power of the Holy Spirit you may abound in hope. Romans 15:13

Hope Notes

*Dedicated to Betty Duda, whose passion
for living, heart for ministry, and zeal for her Lord
are an inspiration to all of us.*

Hope Notes

DEVOTIONS FOR WOMEN

CONCORDIA PUBLISHING HOUSE · SAINT LOUIS

✝ ✝ ✝ ✝ ✝ ✝ ✝ ✝ ✝ ✝ ✝ ✝ ✝ ✝

Table of Contents

✝ ✝ ✝ ✝ ✝ ✝ ✝ ✝ ✝ ✝ ✝ ✝ ✝ ✝

A Letter to the Reader

But I will hope continually and will
praise You yet more and more.

Psalm 71:14

The ladies who wrote these devotions are
connected in a unique way: they share a
common bond because they have all served as
president of the Lutheran Women's Missionary
League (LWML). Their work for the Lord as leaders has been a blessing to the Lutheran Church—
Missouri Synod, to the Church at large, and to
people throughout the world.

Yet they also share a common bond with all of
us who read this book: they, too, are children of
God. They are sisters in Christ. They are women
in mission so that the Good News of Jesus' death
and resurrection for all people may be shared to
the corners of the earth.

As you read these pages, you will find that you
have more in common with these faithful women.
They have known pain and loss. They have known
joy and blessing. They have helped the poor and

lonely. They have found joy in those around them. And through all these stories, you will see that they also share our hope—the hope we have in our God.

We can "hope continually," even in the midst of tragedy. We can "praise [Him] yet more and more," even when we are weary. As you will find in these pages, our hope is not a passing wish or a dim possibility. We have a *certain* hope; we can "abound in hope" (Romans 15:13) because our hope is in the Lord, who never changes, never fails, and never abandons us.

Women of all ages can connect with these women and find encouragement in their words, their stories, and their witness to the Lord.

We serve the Lord in different ways, and our journeys in life take different paths. But through it all, we know that we all share our Savior, our sure hope.

As you learn more about these women, find comfort in their stories and be refreshed by their words as they share with you their hope in our Lord Jesus Christ.

—Lisa Clark

His Healing Hands

Heal me, O LORD, and I shall be
healed; save me, and I shall be saved,
for You are my praise.

Jeremiah 17:14

What causes you to go to God in prayer? When is it essential to turn to the Lord in prayer? Serious illness may be the number one reason for being in earnest prayer, whether it is personal, it affects someone near and dear, or even if it is a request for healing of an acquaintance. We plead. We beg. We want a cure. We want healing. We want that person who means so much to us to be whole again.

A Christian theologian, trained as a medical doctor, has talked and written about the prayer for healing. When cancer strikes or heart disease enfeebles, we ask for healing. We want the subject of that prayer request to get well. We want the person to be free of disease. If we have the choice, we want a return to full health. Are we asking for a cure or for healing? Perhaps the healing comes in a different way. The healing comes in knowing that God is in control and that, in the end, all will be well.

We know that there are times when the disease does not disappear. The patient is finally in hospice care. Our loved one leaves this world. We endure the grief with faith in hope in Christ. But our sorrow turns to hope as we also rejoice that suffering has ended and that heaven is the new home. We have faith in Christ's work on our behalf to bring us to everlasting life.

So has the prayer for healing been answered? Yes. God answers all prayers. It is for us to trust in His answers. He holds us in His hands. Always!

Dear Father, so often, we pray for healing. We want to be well. We want to enjoy this life and all that it has to offer. We want our loved ones to be with us. Help us to accept the healing that You offer. Save us, and we will be saved. In Jesus' name we pray. Amen.

—GE

Where Do Sinners Go?

May our Lord Jesus Christ Himself,
and God our Father, who loved us and
gave us eternal comfort and good hope
through grace, comfort your hearts
and establish them in every good work
and word.

2 Thessalonians 2:16–17

As the pastor was beginning his sermon, he shared a story. Two friends were walking and talking. One was a Christian; the other was uncommitted but interested in spiritual matters. He asked the Christian, "Where do sinners go?" The probable answer would be "to hell." However, the answer came quickly, "Sinners go to church."

What a meaningful answer! All of us are sinners. But because we are living in God's grace, we have forgiveness. And what better place to learn and grow in our faith than by being actively involved in a congregation? It is the place where we can find the assurance of God's forgiveness. In the singing and the sharing, in the message, in the

Confession and Absolution, in coming together at the Lord's Table, it is where encouragement and hope for daily living can be found.

Just what does that look like? Of course, there is Sunday morning worship. And not just attending but also offering assistance wherever needed: ushering, altar care, reading Scripture, singing in the choir, playing bells, teaching Sunday School, bringing snacks for coffee hour, giving monetary support. The list goes on and on. Congregations are always looking for "sinners" to be volunteers to give assistance to give support in deed and word.

All are sinners, but we have forgiveness and the hope of heaven forever with Jesus through the grace of God our Father.

Dear Jesus, we know that You have changed us from a people caught in sin to a redeemed people. Help us to share that with others. Thank You for saving us! In Your name we pray. Amen.

—GE

His Plans for Me

For I know the plans I have for you,
declares the LORD, plans for welfare
and not for evil, to give you a future
and a hope. Then you will call upon
Me and come and pray to Me, and I
will hear you.

Jeremiah 29:11–12

It's a gorgeous blue-sky day. It makes me want
to do something fun. I know there is a long list
of things I should accomplish today. Well, at least
the list is in my head. But maybe I'll go for a walk
first and then read today's paper with another cup
of coffee. I know I should tackle all that work, but
it just seems too much and way too hard. There's
always tomorrow. It won't matter, at least not too
much.

It seems that feeling overwhelmed by circumstances and promises made (mostly to myself)
started long ago. During school years, the start of
every class seemed so exciting. I always thought I'd
get an A. Why not? And then something always got

in the way. Perhaps it was going out with friends or just putting off an assignment. When it wasn't going so well, I must admit, I quit trying very hard.

I've got to remember that God does have plans for me. And yet He forgives me when I sin. Always! All I need to do is ask. I know that He has a purpose for me and that I'm His child. Using my spiritual gifts is not always easy. And I need to ask Him for help in planning my days, fulfilling my roles. I'm going to make a written list. I'm going to tackle all those items, one at a time. With God on my side, I can do it.

One thing is certain: I'm forgiven for past failures. I can count on God's blessings in the future.

Dear Jesus, help me follow Your example of always being on task. Help me plan my day and my future. Help me understand my gifts and use them in service. In Your name I pray. Amen.

—GE

A Hope Unshaken

Our hope for you is unshaken, for
we know that as you share in our
sufferings, you will also share in our
comfort. 2 Corinthians 1:7

Stuff happens, and it happens all the time.
When you listen to the news, when you read the
paper, when you check the Internet, there is often
bad news. It can be very scary, very depressing.
The bad news makes the front page and the lead
story on the evening news. We get instant Internet
reports of shootings and attacks.

Phone calls bring news of illness, accidents,
perhaps even the death of a loved one. Our faith
can be shaken. *Why, God? Why did You take my dad in his
prime? Why does my daughter suffer from leukemia? Why do
I have so many fears?* There's war and disease and
hatred everywhere. It seems to grow and grow.

We know all that happens in today's sinful
world is still under God's control. After all, He
intends all things, even very bad things, for our
good. Good Friday, for example, was a terrible

thing, but our Lord's death on the cross was the way God chose to fulfill His plan for us. It was the absolute worst in exchange for the perfect good. Therefore, we do have victory over suffering, over fears, even over death. We have the great hope of eternal glory. We know that we will live forever, that there will be no more tears, no more hunger, no more death.

It can be very difficult. Every day may seem to be filled with worry and care and, yes, suffering. But we also know that today's suffering is nothing compared to our promised future. We can take great comfort in that. As we put our trust in God to be with us and sustain us, we can live each day fully. We rejoice in knowing that the ultimate victory is ours. Forever and ever!

Father, we give thanks every day for Your good and gracious care. We know that all things work together for good for those who love You. Keep us in Your love. Amen.

—GE

Following the Rules

For through the Spirit, by faith, we
ourselves eagerly wait for the hope
of righteousness. For in Christ Jesus
neither circumcision nor uncircum-
cision counts for anything, but only
faith working through love.

Galatians 5:5–6

Rules, rules, rules! Don't do this, but be sure to
do that. Day in and day out, I try to follow the
law. What I think and what I do are all subject to
rules. The Ten Commandments show me how to
live. "Thou shalt" and "thou shalt not" come at me
from all sides. Some of it is easy, but some—oh, so
difficult.

How can any of us be sure that we have crossed
all the *t*'s and dotted all the *i*'s? After all, nasty
thoughts sneak in at any moment. Try as I might,
I just can't keep myself on an even keel. I get a bit
(or a lot) angry. I feel jealous of my friend or my
neighbor. I don't pay attention during prayer time.
I forget to do my Bible reading. I find it so hard

to apologize. Why do the words "I'm sorry" seem to stick in my throat? What's to come of me? I just can't do it all.

How great is God's love that I, through faith in Jesus, am forgiven. I can count on it. The death and resurrection God's Son promised and delivered gives me freedom to live for Him. Even longed-for righteousness will be mine in eternity!

The gift of faith allows me to actively love. Even though it will not be perfect, I can love myself and love my neighbor. I can live each day in the freedom that comes from faith. Through God's grace, I can live fully and freely. I can love God above all else!

Dear Jesus, forgive my weakness and lack of discipline. Help me to live the life of forgiveness and freedom that You offer. Give me the joy that faith in You brings! In Your name I pray. Amen.

—GE

The Greatest of These Is Love

Love bears all things, believes all
things, hopes all things, endures all
things. . . . So now faith, hope, and
love abide, these three; but the greatest
of these is love.

1 Corinthians 13:7, 13

*L*ove—now *there's* a word. I just told the ladies in
my book club that I loved the last selection. It
was a great read. My boys love the spaghetti and
meatballs I often make. We all love our new puppy.
A young woman I know loves her university.

Certainly, there is love between a husband
and wife. Parents and children love one another,
at least most of the time. The same can be said for
siblings.

We know that God is love. We believe that He
loves us; yes, even us sinners. We know that the
greatest commandment asks us to love God with
all our heart and soul and mind. In our human
condition, we strive to fulfill this command. We
can only because He has forgiven us first.

Then comes the next commandment: love your neighbor as yourself. It's quite clear that we must love ourselves so we can then love others. In many ways, both large and small, love flows from Christ through us to others.

Yet we cannot love—truly love—by our own power. Human love is fickle. But divine love is constant and pure. We can love God and one another only because He loved us first. He loved us to the point of death.

It is because the Holy Spirit created faith in us that we know this. Our faith is in Jesus, our hope is in the resurrection to come, but our love is here and now. God's love surrounds us as we love others. It is a life-changing way to live!

Dear Jesus, we give thanks for our faith. It is a gift from the Holy Spirit. We give thanks for the hope we have in You. Help us grow in our love of You, our neighbor, and ourselves. In Your name we pray. Amen.

—GE

Creator of All Things

By awesome deeds You answer us with
righteousness, O God of our salvation, the hope of all the ends of the
earth and of the farthest seas. . . . The
pastures of the wilderness overflow,
the hills gird themselves with joy,
the meadows clothe themselves with
flocks, the valleys deck themselves with
grain, they shout and sing together
for joy.   Psalm 65:5, 12–13

Oh, what a beautiful world! From the moun-
tains to the seashore, from the plains to the
forests, it is marvelous to behold. Streams flow
and make rivers. They run to the ocean, where
waves dance in the light. Fields are ripe with grain
to nourish and sustain all the people. Hills are
covered in flowers to add beauty to our lives. We
enjoy sunsets and the rise of the full moon. We are
transfixed by millions of stars. Seasons come and
seasons go. The rain falls on the earth to germi-
nate the farmers' seeds. Eventually, there is a har-
vest. We pause and give thanks for our daily bread.

In all this, You, God, are the maker and sustainer of this world and all that is in it. It is Your creation. The intricate design of all that You have created is beyond comprehension.

Everyone and everything everywhere is under Your providence. As believers, we know that not only did You create the world and all that is in it, You have also provided us with the hope of salvation—the ultimate gift! We should dance with joy and sing Your praises. We should shout to all people and share the message of Your love. You have given us so much, especially Your Son, our Savior.

What can we do but offer our gratitude? We offer ourselves to care for the earth and all it holds. Because we have so very much, we reach out to those in need. With Your help, we will tell of Your great love through Jesus, our Lord.

Dear Father, thank You for this world and for the beauty we see every day. Help us share what we have with others, especially the Gospel message of Jesus. Amen.

—GE

Sharing Our Abundance

For the needy shall not always be forgotten, and the hope of the poor shall not perish forever.

Psalm 9:18

Most of us live in the "have" world. It is not easy for us to understand or know what it is like in the "have not" world. Can you imagine putting your children to bed hungry? Do you know what it feels like to get a notice that your electricity will be turned off if you don't pay your overdue bill? Do you ever worry about being homeless? What would it be like to sleep in your car or go to a shelter?

Most of us don't ever face those extreme situations, thanks be to God! Although we might have money worries, we manage to keep food on the table and a roof over our heads. If we get in trouble, we have resources, family, and friends to help us.

For people living in some parts of the United States and for many living in other countries, those "have not" situations are commonplace.

And often, there is little help or hope for change. There is no helping hand.

Martin Luther himself once said, "By faith we receive blessings from above, from God; through love we give them out below, to our neighbor." In fact, he felt that *neighbor* should be translated as "someone in need." That someone can be in our own town or somewhere far away.

Out of our abundance, we can reach out to those who have little. Our heavenly Father blesses us, and we can share with others. There are many avenues for doing that. And not just dollars are important. Our time, our caring attitudes, and our thoughtful response to the poor and needy will make a difference.

Dear Father, thank You for Your abundant blessings. Please give us generous hearts so that we gladly share what You have given us. In Jesus' name we pray. Amen.

—GE

Living Forgiven

Put on then, . . . compassionate
hearts, . . . bearing with one another
and, if one has a complaint against
another, forgiving each other; as the
Lord has forgiven you, so you also
must forgive. Colossians 3:12–13

My infant grandson became very ill with an in-
fection. He was hospitalized and underwent
surgery. At the end of it all, I received a picture
of Paxton sitting in his car seat, ready for the ride
home from the hospital. I shared the picture with
friends. Everyone replied by saying he was cute, he
has beautiful dimples—you know, the loving, fun
compliments. I realized as I read those comments
that I saw a different Paxton in the picture. I saw
eyes that were sparkling without pain or fear, and
a smile that was overjoyed—that said, "I'm healthy,
Grandma!"

As chosen children of God, our Lord sees us
through the cross of His Son, Jesus Christ. He sees
us free and forgiven. Forgiven to live for Him in

everything we do and say. Forgiven to forgive others and to tell them they are forgiven. Forgiven to ask for forgiveness from those we have harmed.

In Colossians 3:13, the Bible tells us, "if one has a complaint against another, [forgive] each other; as the Lord has forgiven you, so you also must forgive." Ask for forgiveness from those you hurt, and speak the words of forgiveness to those who have hurt you. Only through the work of the Holy Spirit can we forgive and be forgiven. We need to remember that we are powerless but that God is all powerful. The results of forgiveness will become clear as we rely on God—Father, Son, and Holy Spirit—to help us make amends with those we have harmed or those who have harmed us.

Dear Father, forgive us our sins, as we forgive those who sin against us. Amen.

—KK

Widow

Fear not, for I am with you; be not
dismayed, for I am your God; I will
strengthen you, I will help you, I will
uphold you with My righteous right
hand. Isaiah 41:10

*M*y world is upside down, spinning out of control! *Every-thing is changing; nothing will ever be the same again!*

Or so I thought.

When I was told that my husband, Mark, had
six to twelve months to live, my world reeled with
confusion and fear of the unknown. As I drove
home after hearing the news, I remember calling
out to God for help. He enabled Scripture verses
to fill my being with comfort and direction:

Isaiah 41:10.

Proverbs 3:5–6.

Psalm 37:7.

Yes, things of this world *were* changing, but
God's Word *never* changes. His promises made

thousands of years ago remain the same, no matter what our circumstances.

As time goes on and I adapt to more changes, God is leading me to take yet another look at my life, life as a widow after forty years of marriage. He brings insight for the day through His Word and the strength and peace that only He can give. He reminds me of His grace and love. He assures me that He has brought me to this new day and He will see me through it. Where is my life going? Wherever that will be, I know I am not alone.

I pray that the joy I have in my Savior and the opportunity to serve Him and His people at this time in my life are reflections of His love for me.

God, You promise to be with us and to strengthen us. Come what may, help us wait patiently and trust in You. In Jesus' name we pray. Amen.

—KK

Better Together

Therefore shall a man leave his father and his mother, and shall cleave unto his wife: and they shall be one flesh.

Genesis 2:24 (KJV)

Marriage is a relationship; marriage is a commitment. A Christ-centered marriage is united in Christ. The Christ-centered marriage is one where both husband and wife are united in Christ. In Genesis (KJV), God tells us that a man will leave his parents and "shall cleave" to his wife. The word *cleave* can mean "be glued." I believe the glue is the commitment, the commitment to work out our problems and to sacrifice for the other; it is going the extra mile and loving each other even when we are unlovable. It is keeping Christ the center of the home.

"Husbands, love your wives, as Christ loved the church and gave Himself up for her" (Ephesians 5:25).

Christ's love for the Church is a perfect love. We are not capable of Christ's perfect love, but because we are children of God and the Holy Spirit has filled us with His gifts, we can speak to each other in kind and loving ways. A Christ-centered marriage has a mutual love and respect that is demonstrated in both word and deed. Be sensitive and attentive to each other's needs. The thoughtful kindness and consideration from day to day strengthens the bonds of love, but sometimes we become so busy with our day-to-day routine that we forget to be kind and considerate.

Ladies, do something special for your husband today, but most of all, pray intentionally for him every day. Remember to tell your spouse you love him, and do kiss him good night. Keep God the center of your relationship, and you will, my friend, be better together!

Loving Lord, thank You for the gift of marriage. Enable us to preserve this gift in our own families and to support the marriages of others. Help us share Your love with one another. Amen.

—KK

The Remote!

Do not be anxious about anything,
but in everything by prayer and supplication with thanksgiving let your
requests be made known to God. And
the peace of God, which surpasses all
understanding, will guard your hearts
and your minds in Christ Jesus.

Philippians 4:6–7

Mark's celebration of life was over, and the house was quiet. After forty years of marriage, I had control of the remote to the television. Mark would have truly enjoyed the moment! My kids laughed; Lexi and Trevor offered to show me how to use it. The problem is that after they have gone home, Grandma forgets! Lexi tells me, "Grandma, just keep punching buttons." Sometimes it's just not worth the hassle.

Philippians 4:6–7 says, "Do not be anxious about anything, but . . . let your requests be made known to God. And the peace of God, which surpasses all understanding, will guard your hearts and your minds in Christ Jesus."

There it is: God's promise. At God's invitation, we take our problems to Him in prayer, and at the same time, thank Him for all the things He has already done for us. Life—and remotes—sometimes do not make sense, but God's grace is always real. God promises to guard my heart and my mind and to give me His peace. Even if I can't use the television remote, the Holy Spirit will lead me to serve our Lord wherever He has need of me!

Father, when life is too hard for us to understand, give us Your peace, which passes our understanding. Guard our hearts and minds in You. Amen.

—KK

Life Out of Control

Come to Me, all who labor and are
heavy laden, and I will give you rest.
Matthew 11:28

Still today I hear the words, smell the antiseptic,
and see the love and respect in the eyes of the
medical staff. Mark's breathing had changed; I see
the nurse making eye contact with my son, Chris,
and son-in-law, Tim; I hear a short, soft sob coming from Chris. As they speak nearly simultane-
ously, I hear Pastor reading Matthew 25:23: "Welcome home! 'Well done, good and faithful servant.
You have been faithful over a little; I will set you
over much. Enter into the joy of your master,'"
and my son softly saying, "Mom . . . he's gone."

This was life out of control for me—but it was
not out of control for our Lord. In His infinite
wisdom and grace, He had everything under control, as He does every day of our lives. Our Lord
allows out-of-control times in our lives but He
does not create them.

Our everyday lives include many out-of-control days. As forgiven children of God, we need to forgive, be patient, and take each day as God gives it to us. He has a plan for each of our lives, and I know His plan is best for each of us!

"Many are the plans in the mind of a man, but it is the purpose of the LORD that will stand" (Proverbs 19:21).

Heavenly Father, our days can become so out of our control. But they are not out of Your control. Guide our days, and give us peace and rest in You. Amen.

—KK

Life's Manuscript

Trust in the LORD with all your heart,
and do not lean on your own understanding. In all your ways acknowledge
Him, and He will make straight your
paths. Be not wise in your own eyes;
fear the LORD, and turn away from
evil.

Proverbs 3:5–7

When I was a young wife and mother, I did lots of reading. I loved historical novels, and my family would often give me books as gifts. They also knew I would always read two or three chapters of a book and then read the last chapter before going back and reading the chapters in between. I'd tell my family that it was because I needed to make sure the book was worth reading!

One Christmas, my sister gave me several books. As I opened my gift, many in my extended family were giggling. I had no idea why a gift of books would be so funny. But I quickly realized my sister had carefully removed the last chapter from each book, and she wasn't about to give them to me until I had read the entire book.

As baptized children of God, our life manuscript is already written and sealed with the blood of Jesus. We know what the last chapter will be: life eternal with our Lord and Savior, Jesus Christ. We do not know what the earlier chapters will bring in our lives, but through the working of the Holy Spirit, we are reminded each day of His love for us.

Each chapter will bring us to a different time in our faith lives. Each chapter will bring us closer to our Lord through joys and sorrows, trials and accomplishments.

O Lord, forgive me when I lean on my own understanding. Direct my paths, and help me to trust in You with my whole heart. Amen.

—KK

Mixed Messages

If any of you lacks wisdom, let him ask
God, who gives generously to all without reproach, and it will be given him.

James 1:5

Have you ever heard someone say, "There are
no stupid questions," only to think, *Then why
am I so afraid to ask one?* In Mark 9, Jesus tells His
disciples of His upcoming death and resurrection,
but for some reason, they didn't understand what
He was trying to tell them. Not only did they not
understand, but they also were afraid to ask Him
what He meant.

Today, where is the first place we go when we
are mixed up about life or are having a problem?
Most people might say that they google it and then
go to family, friends, or anyone else who will listen
as they attempt to talk about their confusion. After
all of the analysis, feedback, and Web surfing, they
will probably have a pile of contradictions and
opinions that they have to sort through instead
of answers.

The devil, the world, and our flesh are all trying to make us crazy, and they send us a lot of mixed messages. The best resources we have in this life for answering our questions aren't people or the Internet. They are prayer and time in God's Word. He promises, "If any of you lacks wisdom, let him ask God" (James 1:5).

Go ahead and ask God anything—He promises to listen! Take your questions and concerns to Him in prayer, knowing that He loves you and that He will never think your questions are stupid or unimportant. Then, be in His Word privately and with other members of the Body of Christ, being blessed by God's counsel, knowing that He doesn't send any mixed messages!

Lord, thank You for Your sure and true Word. Thank You for listening to my prayers and questions. Today, I ask You _____. Amen.

—KK

Going Overboard

[Jesus] called His disciples to Him
and said to them, "Truly, I say to you,
this poor widow has put in more than
all those who are contributing to the
offering box. For they all contributed
out of their abundance, but she out of
her poverty has put in everything she
had, all she had to live on."

Mark 12:43–44

The phrase "going overboard" could be defined by Jesus' words as He describes the poor widow who gave her last mite: "For they all contributed out of their abundance, but she out of her poverty has put in everything she had, all she had to live on." In light of this definition, the good news is that Lutheran Women in Mission, by the grace of God, have "gone overboard" with their mite offerings!

Mother Teresa has said, "It's not how much we give but how much love we put into giving." The love of Christ motivates us to continue to give and support missions. God blesses each of us with gifts of money and gifts of talents. God does not call all of us to be leaders, but He does call us to be faithful in prayer and studying His Word. He calls us to give as the widow did in Mark 12, and He reminds us in Matthew 6:21, "For where your treasure is, there your heart will be also."

Lord, set our hearts on heaven, and focus our time, talents, and treasures on furthering Your kingdom. Forgive us when we fall short, and enable us to "go overboard" in love and service to You and to Your people. Amen.

—KK

Childhood Hope
for a Christmas Present

You will find a baby wrapped in swaddling cloths and lying in a manger.

Luke 2:12

Each Christmas when I was a child living with
my maternal grandparents, my eyes anxiously
looked under the Christmas tree and my heart
eagerly hoped for one present, a gift from my
mother. Usually I was disappointed. However, one
year, I was overjoyed. There were *two* presents—a
doll and a pinkish gold Bulova watch—from my
mother. The gifts told my heart that my mother
loved me. As I got older and realized that the watch
was used, my love of the gift was not adversely
affected. After sixty-plus years, I still have the doll
and the watch.

Have you been disappointed by someone's
actions or lack of action? Have you rejoiced over
an unexpected kind word or compliment?

Even though the two gifts from my mother
are special to me, the most important gift we have

received is the one our heavenly Father gave us in the form of a baby placed in a manger. It was the perfect love gift. God knew exactly what we needed.

What criteria do you use for selecting a gift? Do you spend time on the perfect wrapping?

Although we may keep a Christmas gift for a short time or a long time, once we die, it has no value to us. The gift that God gave us in that manger has value for a lifetime and for all eternity. God wrapped the perfect gift in swaddling cloths.

Dear Lord, help us to share this gift with everyone, because Jesus is the perfect gift. Amen.

—IM

Dee's Hope—Christ

In the same way, let your light shine
before others, so that they may see
your good works and give glory to your
Father who is in heaven.

Matthew 5:16

Each Friday, Dee stood at the counter and sta-
pled the bulletins. After a few weeks in another
state, we returned on a Friday morning to fold
bulletins. Upon entering the church, I saw that
Dee was seated at a church office desk to use the
stapler. Immediately, my heart ached. It meant the
cancer was worse.

Dee had been declared free of breast cancer
for a few years, but the cancer returned in the
pancreas. Her cancer diagnosis did not diminish
her hope in Christ. In fact, it seemed to only
make her more concerned about letting the light
of Christ shine through her.

Because of Dee's love of maintaining the histo-
ry of the Pike's Peak area of Colorado and because

46

of her enthusiasm for collecting and selling antiques, she was known throughout the area.

A baptized daughter of God, Dee had deep compassion for people to know Jesus; she was so willing to let God use her Lutheran education, her love of people, and her access to people to share her faith.

Even though she did not have a husband or children with whom she could share Jesus, she shared Him for years as a college professor. When she retired and returned to her childhood home, she happily and readily let her nieces and nephews and anyone whom the Lord put in her path see Him in her words and actions.

Even as she suffered, God turned tragedy to joy. Dee's final message to her church circle sisters was to ask us to find a Bible verse. In fulfilling her request, we read the words of 1 Corinthians 3:23, "You are Christ's, and Christ is God's."

Dear Lord, help us to let our lights shine for You with others. Amen.

—IM

Hope Chest

> Do not lay up for yourselves trea-
> sures on earth, where moth and rust
> destroy, . . . but lay up for yourselves
> treasures in heaven. . . . For where
> your treasure is, there your heart will
> be also.
>
> Matthew 6:19–21

Do you have a hope chest? Years ago, a hope chest (sometimes called a dowry chest) was an essential piece of furniture for a young woman, especially one who was of marriageable age. Hand-made items such as kitchen, dining, and bed linens, quilts, and the like were put in the chest. The chest was also used to hold her wedding clothes plus other clothing that exhibited her needlework skills. Her hopes for the future were in that chest.

In some areas of the country, a hope chest lined with cedar became necessary to prevent moths and insects from destroying the clothes.

In Matthew 6:20, we read, "Lay up for yourselves treasures in heaven." Have you ever thought of heaven as a very special hope chest that God has made for us?

We can be thankful that we don't have to buy or build or even fill the heavenly hope chest. By grace through faith in Jesus Christ, the Bridegroom is waiting for His Bride and her perfect wedding dress of righteousness. With this wedding, we will be blessed with a future that is beyond our imagination.

Do we spend more time on our earthly hope chest or our heavenly hope chest? When we spend time studying God's Word, worshiping, and praying, we are setting our hearts on God's heavenly hope chest. And even as we do, He is filling us with hope in Christ.

Dear Lord, thank You for preparing heaven, which is no longer a wishful hope but an absolute hope fulfilled. Amen.

—IM

I-Centered Hope
or Christ-Centered Hope?

Now to Him who is able to do far
more abundantly than all that we ask
or think, according to the power at
work within us.

Ephesians 3:20

I hope I get an A on the test.

I hope I get a raise at work.

I hope I get a great gift for my birthday.

I hope someone else will volunteer to teach the second-grade Sunday School class.

I hope Pastor's sermon keeps me awake.

Have you ever let those or similar thoughts go through your mind—or even expressed them out loud to someone?

Probably most of us have done so. Because it is easy to hope for or want things that we desire, our prayer life can become stuck on asking for things. We may even try to make sure He understands exactly why we want something or why we can't do something.

Is our prayer life affected by our I-centered hopes and wants?

With a little checking, we can readily determine if we are in a state of asking for what *we* want or asking God to do that which He knows is best for us. In John 10, Jesus tells us that He is the Good Shepherd. He takes care of us completely. In verse 10, we have the promise that we have life and life to the full. Consider also Ephesians 3:20 (above).

Are we closing our eyes to what God desires to do for us? Just consider John 10 and Ephesians 3:20. God forgives our self-centeredness! Ask the Holy Spirit to help us dwell on Christ and His grace rather than on "I."

Dear Lord, help us to keep our lives centered on Christ, our real hope. Amen.

—IM

God's Hope—Promise Kept

Who shall separate us from the love of
Christ? . . . [Nothing] will be able to
separate us from the love of God in
Christ Jesus our Lord.

Romans 8:35, 39

Today we are bombarded with promises from
commercials, political campaigns, and more.
Because we have "itching ears," we readily want to
believe what we hear. Most often, the promises tell
us that life will be better or that we can have the
desires of our heart.

Even as Christians, we may make promises to
God similar to New Year's resolutions. At first, we
remember and try to fulfill our promises. However, with the passage of time, it becomes difficult to
keep our word due to lack of time, money, and so
on. Of course, we know the real reason is sin. Our
resolution changes from "I promise" to "I may."

But thanks to God, His resolutions are
absolutely certain. His promises are always kept.
Although the words in Romans 8:35–39 are often

used as a funeral text, they are words to keep in our hearts for daily living. In this passage, God tells us that absolutely nothing—tribulation, distress, persecution, famine, nakedness, danger, sword, height, depth, anything in creation—will be able to separate us from the love of Christ.

What does a promise mean to you? Do the words of Romans 8 give you peace of mind and heart?

How blessed we are to know that even if we do not keep our promises to God, God keeps His promises to us. We don't have to hope or wish. God's hope and God's promises are certain.

Dear Lord, help me trust Your promises every day of my life. Amen.

—IM

Hope through Stoplight Prayer

Do not be anxious about anything,
but in everything by prayer and supplication with thanksgiving let your
requests be made known to God.

Philippians 4:6

What is traffic like in your world? If you live in a small town or out in the country, are you able to drive in a relaxed manner? Or do you live in a city where you seem to be traveling through a maze?

Do you pray while driving?

Many years ago, we were in a small-group Bible study. One of the members was a delivery truck driver in a congested city. At each Bible study, an opportunity would afford the friend to express his concern about the traffic and especially about the time spent at stoplights. By the time he got to Bible study, he was exasperated from his job. One night, the group suggested that he use the time while stopped at traffic lights to pray. He took the suggestion to heart and did pray. Regularly, we received reports about his stoplight prayer life for others. He took to heart the words of Ephesians 6:18 by "making supplication for all the saints."

By praying for others at stoplights, our friend was surrounded by peace rather than filled with anxiety, and many were surely blessed by God through his prayers. What times of anxiety in your life could be lessened by prayer? Do you sometimes (as I do) try to handle worries by yourself before you let God give you His certain hope?

We don't have to carry this weight. Jesus is willing to bear it for us, which is what He did! He took the worries and anxieties of the world to the cross. We can take all of our concerns to Him in prayer and be confident that He listens. Prayer—what a blessing the Lord gives us! What a relief!

Dear Lord, help me to pray at all times. Amen.

—IM

Living in Christ's Hope Every Day

> This is the day that the LORD has
> made; let us rejoice and be glad in it.
>
> Psalm 118:24

In a hospital room, a very small two-year-old boy lay with a very serious condition involving the brain. The diagnosis of his situation and the prognosis for the future were in question.

As I traveled to visit the boy's family, my mind was troubled about what I would say or do. Upon arriving at the hospital, I located the boy's mother and gave her a hug and a greeting card with a note. The thought in the card included a Bible verse: Psalm 118:24.

Although the little boy experienced some difficult health issues, including twenty-two shunt revisions during his youth, he grew, was confirmed, and graduated from high school and college. Then, without warning, some twenty-eight years after his first hospital stay, this young man was called home unexpectedly by the Lord.

Of course, we may wonder why the Lord let him live for only thirty years and then took him. Why did he even have a problem in the first place? We can ask why. Even when no answer comes, we are reminded by the Holy Spirit that the great God of hope loves us. And we can be certain that our Lord sympathizes with our grief because He wept with the mourners at Lazarus's tomb. We know the rest of that story too. Jesus raised Lazarus from death and promises that He will raise all who believe in Him as Redeemer and Savior.

We can plan for the future, but this is the day to live for Him. How blessed we are to live every day in the hope of Christ.

Dear Lord, help us to trust and accept Your will for us. May we live every day in Your love, joy, and peace. Amen.

—IM

Our Presence—Present of Encouragement

Therefore encourage one another and
build one another up, just as you are
doing.

1 Thessalonians 5:11

When something we call "good" happens to
us, we want to share the event with others.
When something we call "bad" happens to us, we
may desire the presence of others through a hug,
comforting words, or a greeting card. The other
person's presence in whatever form is a present,
especially in time of need.

Recently, our daughter entered a marathon.
She had previously run a half marathon, but never
a full one, 26.2 miles. As a surprise, her father
and I decided to travel the four hours to attend the
event. We knew our presence would encourage her
to complete the difficult task.

More important than being there for someone's marathon for one day is being there for

others in their daily run with Jesus. One way to help in this journey is to join together in the worship of the Lord. One Sunday, I told a grandson who sat by me in church that his attendance was the best Christmas present he could give to me.

If the thought that you have nothing to give or to receive crosses your mind, think again.

Do you recall a time that you wanted to yell about a happening like an engagement, graduation, or birth of a baby? How about a sad time such as job loss, death, or depression?

Our presence as Christians is needed to mutually encourage one another in times of happiness and sadness. Not only can we be thankful for friends and family who are present for us, we can be certain that Jesus Himself promises "Lo, I am with you always to the end of the age" (Matthew 28:19). What a blessing to have His promised presence in His Word!

Dear Father, help us to encourage others with Your kind words. Amen.

—IM

Hope Comes in Unexpected Ways

Fear not, for I am with you; be not dismayed, for I am your God; I will strengthen you, I will help you, I will uphold you with My righteous right hand. Isaiah 41:10

Hope is a vital necessity of life—a gift that God wants to give to you. In a world that regularly writes dreams off as foolish and drains the hope from the heart with dark pessimism, biblical "hope" is anchored in Christ and His work for me, even if I'm not feeling it at the moment.

One difficult situation that many of us never may have experienced is prison. Recently, a friend from our church started doing prison ministry at our local correctional facility with Eddie, our comfort dog from Lutheran Church Charities.

Eddie and two of his handlers had previously gone to the facility to receive permission to visit the inmates. The administration of the facility was open to it, but they held back any hope that this would be a good idea for the inmates, or even for Eddie.

However, with permission granted, Eddie and his handlers were on their way! After several visits, they received this note from an inmate: "Thank you so much for that comforting and supportive opportunity." The officer in charge of the female unit told the handlers she saw a transformation after an inmate returned from her interaction with Eddie and the handlers.

So often when we use the word *hope* in casual conversation, it has a wavering, uncertain sound. Most people live in hope that things will get better, that things will improve for them, and that they will be satisfied. The world hopes for the best, but Jesus Christ offers the best hope—mercy and the promise of heaven. A hope that is certain!

Father, give hope to those who live in difficult situations. Help me to bring God's love to them. Amen.

—LR

Reward to Come

Preparing your minds for action, and
being sober-minded, set your hope
fully on the grace that will be brought
to you at the revelation of Jesus Christ.

1 Peter 1:13

Trips to town to sell eggs. Trips to town to visit
Grandma. Trips to town to get some needed
supplies. Growing up, I was blessed to have many
opportunities to spend time with "older adults,"
and I learned to enjoy and appreciate their com-
pany and their stories. Many times on our trips to
town, we would visit Great-Aunt Marie, who had
been a widow for many years and yet lived in and
maintained her own home. Dad was a "handyman"
and often would be requested to fix this or repair
that while Mom and we kids enjoyed cookies in the
house. I always recall Great-Aunt Marie's thought-
fulness to my parents after they helped her with a
task, repair, or project. She would say, "You will
get your reward someday."

At the time, I did not fully appreciate or understand the meaning of that phrase. I always thought she would someday monetarily reward my parents. She often did invite us to enjoy some of her delicious *ebelskiver* (Danish pancake) dinners, where my brother and I would see who could devour the most! However, what I later learned from this wonderful Christian woman is that the greatest gift we have is the reward we will receive someday because of the grace and mercy of our Lord and Savior, Jesus Christ.

It is easy to seek rewards here on earth. It is easy to want compensation for work we believe is worthy of such. It is easy to expect earthly rewards to show the value of something we have done. However, our hope, our reward, is in the person of Jesus Christ and His promise for our future.

Dear Lord, I thank You for the gift of faith in Jesus as my Savior. May my words and actions reflect the glory You deserve. In His precious name I pray. Amen.

—LR

Leaping in Faith

Now faith is the assurance of things hoped for, the conviction of things not seen. Hebrews 11:1

I recently had the opportunity to witness the amazing African impala in its native environment. This animal is comparable to our native pronghorn antelope. The word *amazing*, however, has to be used for the African impala because these creatures can jump to a height of more than ten feet and, in a single leap, cover a distance greater than thirty feet. Yet impalas can be kept inside a zoo enclosure by a simple three-foot wall. Why? Impalas will not jump if they can't see where their feet will land.

Do we have something in common with these antelopes? Are we able to take great leaps of faith, but refuse to do so unless we can see where we'll land?

True faith cannot see how the landing will occur; it simply leaps under the conviction that it *will* occur. Our faith and hope are never in vain

64

because they are in a God who is faithful to His promises. Remember, biblical faith begins where our power ends. Enjoy the leap!

Dear Father, thank You for Your protection and promise of hope from now through eternity. Amen.

—LR

Singing Birds

I wait for the LORD, my soul waits, and in His word I hope. Psalm 130:5

As a child growing up on the farm, I would sometimes just lie in bed on spring and summer mornings with the windows open, listening to the birds begin their singing. I often wondered why they sang and what they were singing about. I often tried to imitate their song, and I was thrilled if they seemed to respond to my childish whistle.

I was told they might sing because they were happy to see the sun again! However, the funny thing is that I was able to witness that the singing started long before the sun was visible. And yet they sang anyway. They sang in the darkness because they knew it wouldn't stay dark forever.

In our lives and in our world today, we experience darkness around us. We know that our sin has separated us from God, but with Christ Jesus, we were brought out of darkness through Christ, the light of the world.

In Psalm 130, the psalmist captures the essence of our God's love for us. Christ has eradicated our sins; He has given us a complete cure. While we wait for our final deliverance from this life to eternity, knowing we have been cured, we can sing our praise and thanks to Him who has put the song in our heart.

Sing to welcome the sun, even if you cannot quite see it yet.

O Lord God, I thank You for the gift of song, for Your gift of listening, for knowing me, and for always being there to answer. In Jesus' name I pray. Amen.

—LR

Hope Is Found in Jesus

Blessed be the God and Father of our Lord Jesus Christ! According to His great mercy, He has caused us to be born again to a living hope through the resurrection of Jesus Christ from the dead. 1 Peter 1:3

Imagine with me that your child is lost in a large crowd of people. Suddenly you realize the child is not with you. It recently happened to our family with one of our grandchildren. Fortunately, the child was quickly found and all was well. However, it made me realize that we would have searched relentlessly to find this child; we would not have quickly given up hope in that search.

Like a child separated from parents, our sin separates us from God. Romans 3:23 says we "all have sinned and fall short of the glory of God." That sounds utterly hopeless, but like the family who will not give up looking for their child, God found a way to repair our relationship with Him.

Through His Son, Jesus, God made a way for us to have a relationship with Him. Jesus is the object and source of our hope. This is why Jesus coming down to earth on Christmas is so important. Without Jesus' birth, death, and resurrection, our sins would not be forgiven. We would still be apart from God, like a child lost in a crowd.

Jesus brings hope to all areas of our lives. There is no situation in your life right now that is too bad for the "living hope" promised to us in I Peter 1:3. We celebrate Christmas because it is all about hope, and that hope would not be possible without Jesus.

Loving Father, give us a sure, certain, and living hope in You and Your promises to us, that we may always trust in You. In Your Son's name we pray. Amen.

—LR

Such a Time as This

But I will hope continually and will
praise You yet more and more.

Psalm 71:14

We are living in a time of terrorism and ter-
rorists! Daily, we can read in our newspapers
and see on our televisions these acts of violence
and the fear they create. We can also read in the
Book of Esther words that were spoken by Morde-
cai to Esther after she became queen: "Who knows
whether you have not come to the kingdom for
such a time as this?" (4:14).

As we serve our Lord and His people, we
should ask ourselves this question: Who knows?
Perhaps it is for a time like this that our Lord is
asking us to serve! In order to serve our Lord and
share His message in a sin-sick world at "such a
time as this," we need to rely on Proverbs 3:5,
"Trust in the LORD with all your heart, and do not
lean on your own understanding."

We are living in a time when we see people
placing trust in their bank accounts, in the govern-

ment, or even in their family and friends. These often disappoint. Yes, sometimes we trust in the wrong things! *Trust in the Lord with all your heart, and do not lean on your own understanding.*

Perhaps there are other obstacles in our lives that keep us from placing our complete trust and hope in God. Martin Luther said it best in the Small Catechism: "We should fear, love, and trust in God above all things" (explanation of the First Commandment)!

As we continue our journeys of faith, we put our hope and trust in our great God, who gave us His perfect love in the person of His Son, Jesus, so that His healing love can now be extended to others through us.

Gracious God, heavenly Father, thank You for allowing me to come into Your presence at any time, to know hope and trust through You! Amen.

—LR

Calming Our Life Storms

Let us hold fast the confession of our hope without wavering, for He who promised is faithful.

Hebrews 10:23

If there is one positive thing that hurricanes, tsunamis, tidal waves, and tornadoes have done, it is cause people to think. Some may wonder, *Why did God let these storms happen?*

Remember, all creation was affected by the fall. The Scriptures tell us that there will always be upheaval in nature, wars and rumors of war, pain, suffering, and physical death. These events are all results of sin in the world and are reminders that man cannot control all of creation.

Storms get our attention and help us change our focus to the important things of life. Relationships with family and others can be strengthened. Most important, our relationship with and faith in our triune God is stimulated, for only He is the author and finisher of life. Not only does He rescue physically, but He also has provided the ultimate rescue from sin, eternal death, and the devil.

Storms cannot separate us from the love of God. Remember, disruption only takes place during life temporal. God assures us that it will not happen in the new heaven and earth He reveals to us in Revelation.

You do not have to face any of life's storms alone! Our triune God calms all storms in life (Psalm 107:28–31).

Dear Father, Creator God, thank You not only for Your gift of creation, but also for Your faithfulness to uphold us and sustain us through all life's storms because of Jesus, our hope and our rescue. Amen.

—LR

Rest Comes from Him

Come to Me, all who labor and are
heavy laden, and I will give you rest. .
. . You will find rest for your souls.
Matthew 11:28–29

Look at your calendar. Are holidays just around the corner? Are the plans for those holidays looming large in your thoughts and plans? Are the words *holidays* and *weary* synonymous in your thinking? Have you ever been so tired that when you finally got to bed, you could not quiet your mind enough to go to sleep? Being "weary" is not the same as being physically tired. "Weary" is being worn out physically, mentally, and spiritually. "Weary" is being resigned to feeling tired and discouraged and burdened on an ongoing basis.

And this is when Jesus speaks to us, as He always does, in His Word. There He offers peace for the restless and rest for the weary. "Come unto Me," He says, "all you who are weary and burdened"—and that means everyone. It means you,

and it means me, not only if we are weary and burdened by monumental issues or serious problems,
but also whatever our burdens, real or imagined.
He assures us, "I will give you rest"—and not only
rest for our bodies; more important, He says He
will give "rest for your souls."

> I heard the voice of Jesus say,
> "Come unto Me and rest;
>
> Lay down, thou weary one,
> lay down Thy head upon My breast."
>
> I came to Jesus as I was, So weary,
> worn, and sad;
>
> I found in Him a resting-place,
> And He has made me glad.
>
> (*LSB* 699:1)

Dear Gracious God, thank You for the
rest You provide when I am weary. Help
me to cast my cares and burdens on You
and to trust in Your mercy, love, and
grace to provide rest for my soul. Amen.

—LR

Shoes of Healing

For I know the plans I have for you,
declares the LORD, plans for welfare
and not for evil, to give you a future
and a hope.

Jeremiah 29:11

The word *hopeless* comes to mind in this instance. As a registered nurse and as a mom, I've been involved in several hopeless situations.

After the death of our thirty-seven-year-old daughter, I asked her husband for the first thing he'd like me to do on that particularly hopeless morning. His answer: "Clean out the closet, and remove her shoes."

I didn't question him; I just went to work sorting and saving. Slowly, surely, the pile filled a large garbage bag. Who would receive these shoes? The only person who could possibly wear them was her little sister, living in another state—the grieving sister who simply hadn't accepted her sister's early and untimely death.

A few months later, her father and I took the bulging bag of shoes to Colorado, where Susan lived. She was puzzled at the sight of us on the steps with a big bag, looking like Santa Claus himself. We assured her it was a gift, to be used as a reminder of her sister's love and of the healing we all have in Jesus. Her sister's shoes did prove to be a gift of hope; once in a while, I'd see her wearing a pair, sporting them with love and telling whoever would listen, "These were my sister's." The shoes probably healed her heart, as they did mine when I was sorting and saving. Sometimes, what looks or feels like a hopeless situation turns out to be good, all with the help of God.

We know that God has plans for our good. It may involve some unexpected gifts, such as shoes, but He lovingly guides us to find our hope in Him.

Dear Lord, thank You for the gift of hope, given in a bag of sixty pairs of shoes—gifts of love for a needy soul. Help us share our hope in You through whatever means You give us to use. Amen.

—VVS

Baptismal Blessings

Is not your fear of God your confidence, and the integrity of your ways
your hope? Job 4:6

My dad always told me to be confident and
to uphold the integrity of our name. Good
advice for anyone, isn't it?

We are not just a Social Security number.

We are not just a name on a passport, even if
that document is one of our most treasured pos-
sessions.

Our most important certificate is our baptismal certificate, which signifies that we have been
given the gift of the Holy Spirit and that our name
has been entered into the book of heaven.

I always wondered why my parents waited until
I was two years old to take me to the Lord and receive the gift of Holy Baptism. This was a conversation I never had with my parents, and now that
they are gone to heaven, I wish I could. My own
solution is that I don't think they were churched

before then. When a Lutheran pastor moved to my hometown, it may be that they sought membership in the church and brought me to Baptism. For that, I'm most grateful.

My husband and I brought our three children to Baptism before they were two months old. That provides sure hope that they are children of God, both now and into eternity. It has been the same with grandchildren; all are baptized and assured of God's presence in their lives.

Find your baptismal certificate and have it framed. Hang it in a prominent place in your home, where you can rejoice daily in the blessings of your Baptism.

Dear Father in heaven, thank You for the gift of Baptism, providing life and hope on a daily basis. In Jesus' holy name. Amen.

—VVS

Helping the Hopeless

Do not be anxious about anything,
but in everything by prayer and supplication with thanksgiving let your
requests be made known to God.

Philippians 4:6

It is hard to imagine living on the streets in all
kinds of weather, literally begging for food and
drink. But people do.

One of the jobs I had was at a social service
agency in a large city. Commonly, several of the
homeless would come to the hallway connecting
our offices to the outside world. There they could
"by chance" use the restroom facilities or perhaps
get warm. Once in a while, some of our lunches
would go missing. This occurred more frequently,
of course, during the winter months.

One day, I came face-to-face with the "thief"
of my lunch in the break room. He made a fast
getaway with the evidence, but not before I saw the
look in his eyes: utter hopelessness. His eyes were

dull with it. I felt great sorrow for this young man and for his situation in life.

Shortly afterward, a picture of this same person appeared in the local newspaper, after he had been involved in the accident with a train that took his life. It identified him as the son of a Lutheran pastor. No wonder he had come to the office of a Lutheran social service agency. It left me feeling as if we had failed; that we could have done more. I resolved then, to try to be Jesus' hands and feet and to show compassion and help others when and where I could.

Jesus saw our utter hopelessness and felt such great sorrow for us that He took all of our sins on Himself. His death on the cross was the solution to our hopelessness. Never failing us, He fulfills every need and promises us an eternal home with Him. Alleluia!

Dear Lord, show me ways I can offer hope in material ways and by witnessing to Your mercy and grace. I ask this in Jesus' name.

—VVS

Showing Hope through Care

Love bears all things, believes all
things, hopes all things, endures all
things. 1 Corinthians 13:7

Characteristics of caring—love, joy, peace,
patience, kindness, goodness, faithfulness,
gentleness, self-control—are gifts to us from the
Holy Spirit. We receive these gifts through Baptism. For any Christian nurse, there are opportunities every day to use these gifts in service to
others. Especially if you work in an oncology unit,
or if a family member at home has been given a
diagnosis such as cancer.

A joyful attitude and a smile will go a long way.
Sharing the idea that you have hope and will never
give up is contagious. Belief and faith in the One
who is directing your care will give you peace of
mind every day!

A touch of a hand, assurance that you really
are interested in their well-being, will serve you
well. Knowledge of the diagnosis and participation

in the decision making will also help the family members who are seeking your advice.

If you are the patient, surround yourself with positive people and those who can give you hope in all kinds of situations.

Seek the advice and counsel of your pastor, who will pray for you daily!

Dear Lord, please give us the strength to help others take care of loved ones. Let us have a positive attitude in daily care, focused on the hope we have in You. We ask this in Jesus' name. Amen.

—VVS

Giving Hope, Near and Far

For You, O Lord, are my hope, my
trust, O LORD, from my youth.

Psalm 71:5

My husband and I were privileged to travel to
Africa in 2006, and one of the places we'll
never forget is a camp in West Africa where refu-
gees were housed temporarily. Of course, we had
no idea what to expect, and it was all a surprise
to us.

We saw a church primarily made from World
Relief tarps, and the most astonishing part was the
people inside. Those people had hope that we were
going to help provide a better place of worship for
them.

Another memory is a group of school-age
children in their school uniforms, surrounding
my six-foot five-inch husband. No doubt they had
never seen a white man before, but they began
walking with him, grabbing onto his hand, and
just simply begging for a touch, a word, or a hug.

Their eyes were full of hope! Their big eyes were full of wonder and anticipation for a new beginning. One of my favorite photos is of this very tall white man surrounded by at least a dozen little African boys—all with smiles on their faces!

God uses all of us to touch the lives of others—near and far—sharing the hope of our loving Savior.

Dear Lord, we ask that you give us a world of peace and joy, free from disease and war. Provide people in all war-torn countries with food, medicine, and beds to sleep on. Provide those who are in need with Your all-encompassing love. In Jesus' name we pray.

—VVS

Hope through Prayer

I wait for the LORD, my soul waits, and
in His word I hope. Psalm 130:5

Some days, my own personal idea of what hope
really is can vary. Chances are, you have similar
thoughts.

I hope (wish) it would be nice tomorrow and
quit raining.

I hope (wish) I have enough supplies on hand
in my own kitchen to make this meal.

I hope (really wish) this cold will end soon.

I hope (wish) nothing more will prevent us
from visiting grandkids in another state because
I want to go soon, *and very soon.*

I hope (wish) I know how to do this job
because nothing has prepared me to take it to
completion.

We all have had similar thoughts in our past—
just admit it! We can control those feelings of
inadequacy somewhat by simply preparing for the

situation. I can do my grocery shopping and be ready for the recipe; I can make adequate vacation preparations to make definite plans; and I can study or prepare fully for that new job.

Some things are definitely out of our control. I can't determine the weather, and I can't determine exactly when my illness, no matter how severe, will end. But pray . . . I can do that! I can ask God for favorable weather conditions and for good health to return. That *is* in my control, and I will do that!

I do have confidence—and that's true hope— that the Lord will give me all that I need, especially the hope of His peace and mercy.

Dear Lord in heaven, thank You for Your continued gift of good health and a good understanding of what is needed for a happy life. Thank You for all You've given me and my loved ones in the past and certainly today! We thank and praise You daily. In Jesus' name we pray.

—VVS

Gentle Reminders of Hope

Rejoice in hope, be patient in tribulation, be constant in prayer.

Romans 12:12

Those are big words, "be patient in tribulation" and "rejoice in hope."

As a nurse, I always admire the pastors who can make hospital calls and immediately give hope to families just by their presence in the room.

It's usually done in a very calm manner, quietly, and is perhaps nothing more than a prayer, a presence, and a quiet hug to someone who really needs it.

Some can do this also by just standing there and listening. A smile, a prayer, and promises of hope—usually from the Psalms—are just what family members need when they are in desperate need of hope. Their presence alone can assure the patient that God is with them.

There is usually none of the "rejoicing" as you might think of, with cheers and such, but in some instances, there is. A baby is born, a life is spared, someone survives—there are many situations when everyone is happy and relieved. In others situations, by his mere presence, participating with the family in times of great stress, a pastor participates in a gentle, quiet imparting of hope being given to all in the room.

In those instances, I've been moved to tears many a time by listening to a simple prayer or a quiet reading chosen for the situation, and by the mere fact that the pastor is there. He is with the family, representing Jesus as he speaks the Word, and that is all that is needed.

Dear Lord, thank You for the gift of pastors who bring comforting words and Your Word. It is all gift-wrapped in hope, a special gift to be given to those in need. In Jesus' name I pray. Amen.

—VVS

An Example of Hope

But I will hope continually and will
praise You yet more and more.

Psalm 71:14

Some of my favorite stories of hope experiences
are from patients residing in nursing facilities. One of my favorites comes with a lady I'll call Sylvia, a faithful LWML woman who lived in a care facility close to her home. She was tired of keeping up her home by herself. Work of this kind was hard for her to do in the late stages of her life. Extended family lived nearby, but her pastor son lived in another state, far from her home. It was time to make a change in lifestyle.

I worked in this care facility and visited Sylvia quite often, just to check on her needs and to visit and chat. She had her mite box on the shelf by her Bible, and she kept her sewing machine and quilting supplies nearby so she could continue her hobby, making quilts for Lutheran World Relief.

Most times, she liked me to read an article from the LWML *Quarterly* for her, and I would do that. We'd pray, we'd sing, and once or twice I watched her quilt or piece her quilt blocks. It was easy to see that Sylvia was busy so I kept my visits short. She was happy, content, and most of all, she was full of hope for an eternity in heaven. One day, I took a photo of her quilting with her *Quarterly* by her side and sent it to the *Quarterly* staff for publication. They published it, but by then, she'd forgotten that I'd taken the picture, so she was surprised to see it in print!

Shortly afterward, Sylvia passed away, and our visits here on earth were over. She taught me to appreciate what I have and to be confident in God's love. Her life of hope in Jesus was a blessing to those who witnessed it. And I'm confident that her hope of heaven has been realized.

Dear Lord and Father in heaven, thank You for Your promise of eternal life. Thank You for the gift of the young and the elderly, full of hope in You. In Jesus' name. Amen.

—VVS

Good Hope Road

For You, O Lord, are my hope, my
trust, O LORD, from my youth.

Psalm 71:5

When we moved to the Milwaukee area in
Wisconsin, I couldn't help but notice the
name of one of the major thoroughfares north of
the city: Good Hope Road. I thought it was a nice-
enough name and never thought much about how
that name came to be.

Research on the Internet stated that it was
named for the community of Good Hope, where
European immigrants settled in the 1800s. They
were in search of new land, new possibilities and
purpose, religious freedom, and their own definition of "good hope."

In Christ Jesus, God has given us many things.
First and foremost, He has given us eternal life and
a home in heaven. Because Jesus paid the price for
our sins, we have complete forgiveness and will live
with Him for all eternity.

Our life has new purpose and possibility as we live as His redeemed and dearly loved daughters. Do you ever think of yourself as a princess? Our Father is the King of kings and Lord of lords! As His daughters, we are truly princesses, better than any Disney princess.

True religious freedom has also been won by Him. That doesn't mean we won't have trials or tribulations. Jesus told His disciples and us in John 16:33, "In the world you will have tribulation. But take heart; I have overcome the world." And that, my dear sisters, is the only true "good hope" there is for time and eternity.

Thanks be to You, dear God. You have provided the good hope that I have in Jesus Christ. You, O Lord, are my hope and my trust. Amen.

—JW

Traveling Light

In your hearts honor Christ the Lord
as holy, always being prepared to make
a defense to anyone who asks you for a
reason for the hope that is in you; yet
do it with gentleness and respect.

1 Peter 3:15

While traveling as LWML president, I was often on the road with my suitcase(s) and briefcase filled to overflowing. It seemed I needed to bring my closet and my desk to each meeting and event. I never did learn to travel light. But I did find that it gave me an opportunity to witness, as I often commented, "The only time I will travel light is when I go to heaven, because I won't need any of this there!" It may be one of my favorite "one-liners." It gave me an easy way to share God's love and, most important, the hope that I have in Jesus Christ. Some people responded, "I will see you there!"

I remember one man who asked me if I was sure that I was going to heaven. I answered, "I am, because of Jesus Christ and what He did for me and for all who believe. My sins are forgiven, and I will live eternally with Him in heaven." This man was not sure about his eternal home, and then he told me he really did not want to hear about it. Although he worked at a hotel where I often stayed, our paths never crossed again. My prayer is that other people were able to share their hope with this man too.

Is there some easy, natural way that you, too, can share "the hope that is in you"? Do you have a personal "one-liner" that invites a witness?

Holy Lord Christ, prepare me to share the hope that is in me and to do it with gentleness and respect. Amen.

—JW

Recombobulation Area

The steadfast love of the LORD never ceases; His mercies never come to an end; they are new every morning; great is Your faithfulness. "The LORD is my portion," says my soul, "therefore I will hope in Him."

Lamentations 3:22–24

A few years ago, a sign appeared at General Mitchell International Airport in Milwaukee, Wisconsin, just past the security checkpoint. The sign read, "Recombobulation Area." It was a creative name for the area where travelers who had been "discombobulated" could regroup, gather their belongings, put their shoes and belts back on, and proceed to their gates. One passenger said, "I've seen plenty of discombobulation areas." He was talking both about airport travel and life.

One group voted *recombobulation* the most creative new word of 2008, and it is now listed in some dictionaries. What started out as a joke has become a permanent fixture of our vocabulary.

What is my "recombobulation area"? Where do I go to regroup when things have gone wrong in my life and when there is, indeed, much discombobulation?

God has given me His Word, full of His promises and truths. It is always available to me, along with many study helps and resources. His mercies are new every morning; His faithfulness is great.

He also blesses me in Word and Sacrament. He reminds me that He has called me and sealed me in Baptism. In Holy Communion, He assures me that all my sins are forgiven and He strengthens me with His body and blood, given for me.

God has also given me the Body of Christ, fellow believers who encourage me, lift me up in prayer, and bless me, often just when I need it.

Jesus Christ is my recombobulation area!

Thank You, Lord, for Your steadfast love, Your mercies, and Your great faithfulness. My hope is in You alone. Amen.

—JW

Yours for the Asking

May the God of hope fill you with all
joy and peace in believing, so that by
the power of the Holy Spirit you may
abound in hope.

Romans 15:13

It had been a long, tiring trip on a chartered
bus. Traffic was congested, and we were further
delayed by a multicar accident. Checking into
the hotel room after 11 p.m., I barely noticed my
surroundings; I longed to wash my face, brush my
teeth, and get a few hours of sleep before the meeting scheduled for the next morning.

On the counter in the bathroom, there was a
small sign that read, "Yours for the Asking: just
call the front desk." On it were listed fifteen items
that hotel guests could secure just by calling the
front desk. I had never seen so many items offered
for free! It seemed that someone had thought of
just about everything a traveler might forget or
need. Talk about exceeding expectations—all of

those options, available if or when I needed them, just by placing a call!

Our loving God has thought of everything that you and I need for this life and for eternity—the free gift of life in Christ through faith. He has given us the fruit of the Spirit: love, joy, peace, patience, kindness, goodness, faithfulness, gentleness, and self-control (Galatians 5:22–23). The best part is that we didn't have to do anything; Jesus Christ has done it all, and He freely gives these gifts to each of us. He desires to fill us with all joy and peace in believing, so that we may abound in hope.

Thank You, Lord Jesus. Fill me with Your joy and peace so that I, too, may abound in hope, as Your Word says. Amen.

—JW

The Hope of Eternal Life

In hope of eternal life, which God, who never lies, promised before the ages began . . . Titus 1:2

One practice I have had over the years is keeping a daily calendar. Most years, I choose one with Bible verses; some years, I have used "secular" ones done by an artist whose illustrations are favorites of mine. I also have some perpetual calendars that can be used for any year.

While serving as LWML president, I often came across verses that would supplement my daily quiet time or provide additional material for presentations that I was preparing. At times, I mail the daily tear-off page to a friend, especially if it ministers to a need she has. I have also taped pages into a wire-bound notebook that I use as a makeshift journal.

In many ways, God uses these verses and sayings to encourage and bless me in my daily walk with Jesus. The calendar verse for October 22 was "in hope of eternal life, which God, who never lies, promised before the ages began" (Titus 1:2).

October 22 was my mother's birthday; the day I read it would have been my mother's 98th birthday. She has been celebrating birthdays in heaven since the Lord called her home a few weeks before her 86th birthday.

How grateful I am to God for this word of encouragement on that day—the hope of eternal life, which God has promised before the ages began. God, who never lies, is the one who promised life to all who believe in Jesus as their Lord and Savior.

Thank You, Lord, for memories of loved ones. Most of all, thank You for Your promise, the hope of eternal life. Amen.

—JW

I Hope in Him

The steadfast love of the LORD never ceases; His mercies never come to an end; they are new every morning; great is Your faithfulness. "The LORD is my portion," says my soul, "therefore I hope in Him."

Lamentations 3:22–24

Happy New Year! Now, don't quickly pass over this devotion if it isn't the beginning of January! One has to admit, there is something about that new calendar signifying a brand-new year, something that often inspires people to make resolutions that may go unfulfilled.

A new year is also a time for remembering the past and reflecting on the future. Isaac Watts wrote these words: "O God, our help in ages past, Our hope for years to come, Our shelter from the stormy blast, And our eternal home" (*LSB* 733:1). All of our remembrances rest in the hands of the Lord Almighty, our help in ages past, our hope for years to come, and our eternal home.

With the passing of time, some things come to an end, and changes occur. There is one thing that will never change: our eternal God. We take refuge in His loving arms, relying on His steadfast love that endures forever. That love was made manifest in Jesus Christ, for you and for me. His mercies are new every day, not just on January 1. His faithfulness is great. We can join with the prophet Jeremiah: "The steadfast love of the LORD never ceases; His mercies never come to an end; they are new every morning."

Each day, we can place our hope in Jesus, thanking Him for the forgiveness won for us on Calvary. Each day is a blessed new day in Him!

Lord God, thank You for blessing me with a fresh start each day in You. Amen.

—JW

I Hope in Your Word

You are my hiding place and my
shield; I hope in Your word.

Psalm 119:114

While serving as president of the Lutheran
Women's Missionary League, I shared a
vision that the organization would be known as
Lutheran Women in Mission who are in the Word,
of the Word, and walking with the Word made
flesh, Jesus Christ. Women were encouraged to
honor a daily appointment with the Father and
His Word. This living Word empowers us and
has application in our daily lives. Our hope is
strengthened and nurtured as we read God's Word.
This hope helps us when times are hard, not because things will turn out the way we want them to,
but because our God is absolutely worthy of trust.

Walking with the Lord, we are assured of His
promise never to leave us or forsake us. "It is
the LORD your God who goes with you. He will not
leave you or forsake you" (Deuteronomy 31:6).
God promises, "I will never leave you nor forsake

you" (Hebrews 13:5). We also have the promise of Jesus Christ that He will be with us always, even to the end of the age (Matthew 28:20). Our hope is in Jesus Christ, in His birth, life, death, resurrection, and His promise to come again.

Leaning on Jesus, we walk with Him daily as He directs our steps. Where is your walk taking you?

Lord Jesus, remind me that You walk with me; keep me mindful of Your presence. I hope in Your Word. Amen.

—JW

Lovely to Look At?

I wait for the LORD, my soul waits,
and in His word I hope.   Psalm 130:5

Driving up to our home that December, one
would have believed that we had it all together. The outside of our home was beautiful. Lights
twinkled in the shrubs next to the door, a spotlight
shone on the white cutout nativity scene, and an
elegant wreath was placed on the front door.

One step inside told a different story! New
flooring was being installed, and there was a
problem with the product that had been sent.
Our installer was waiting to hear back from the
manufacturer, and so there we were, with bare
subfloors, furniture crammed into the two rooms
that were not getting new flooring, and nowhere
to put the tree or any interior decorations!

No matter how nice things looked on the
outside, our home inside was chaos, brokenness,
and, quite frankly, a mess. There was nothing we
could do about it until the installer came back to
complete the job.

There is nothing that I can do about my sinful condition either. No matter how good I might look on the outside, inside is chaos, brokenness, and a mess. Only Jesus Christ can come and make things right in my heart and in my life. Jesus has completed the job of my salvation in His death on Calvary and His resurrection. This same Jesus has said, "Behold, I am making all things new" (Revelation 21:5)!

Today, as you encounter people that the Lord places in your path, look beyond the outer facade and pray for opportunities to share the hope you have in Jesus.

Lord, thank You that You take my brokenness and sin and cleanse me from within, giving me hope in Your Word. Amen.

—JW

�֊ �֊ ✖֊ ✖֊ ✖֊ ✖֊ ✖֊ ✖֊ ✖֊ ✖֊ ✖֊ ✖֊ ✖֊

My Hope Notes

_____

_____

_____

_____

_____

_____

_____

_____

_____

_____

_____

_____

_____